THE PRINCETON PRINCIPLES ON UNIVERSAL JURISDICTION

PRINCETON PROJECT ON UNIVERSAL JURISDICTION

Steering Committee

Stephen Macedo, Project Chair
Laurance S. Rockefeller Professor of Politics and The University Center for Human Values; Founding Director, Program in Law and Public Affairs, 1999-2001, Princeton University

Gary J. Bass
Assistant Professor of Politics and International Affairs, Princeton University

William J. Butler
Former Chairman, Executive Committee of the International Commission of Jurists, 1975-1990; President, American Association for the International Commission of Jurists

Richard A. Falk
Albert G. Milbank Professor of International Law and Practice, Professor of Politics and International Affairs, Princeton University

Cees Flinterman
Professor of Human Rights, Utrecht University; Director of the Netherlands Institute of Human Rights and the Netherlands School of Human Rights Research

Bert B. Lockwood
Distinguished Service Professor of Law; Director of the Urban Morgan Institute for Human Rights; University of Cincinnati College of Law

Stephen A. Oxman
Board of Directors, American Association for the International Commission of Jurists; Former U.S. Assistant Secretary of State for European and Canadian Affairs

THE PRINCETON PRINCIPLES ON UNIVERSAL JURISDICTION

With a Foreword by Hon. Mary Robinson
United Nations High Commissioner for Human Rights

Princeton Project on Universal Jurisdiction

SPONSORING ORGANIZATIONS

Program in Law and Public Affairs
and
Woodrow Wilson School of Public and International Affairs
Princeton University

International Commission of Jurists

American Association for the International Commission of Jurists

Netherlands Institute of Human Rights

Urban Morgan Institute for Human Rights

~

Stephen Macedo, Project Chair and Editor

~

Program in Law and Public Affairs
Princeton University ~ Princeton, New Jersey

Copyright © 2001 by
Program in Law and Public Affairs and
Woodrow Wilson School of Public and International Affairs, Princeton University
International Commission of Jurists
American Association for the International Commission of Jurists
Netherlands Institute of Human Rights
Urban Morgan Institute for Human Rights
All rights reserved. Published 2001
Printed in the United States of America

Additional copies may be obtained upon request from:
    Program in Law and Public Affairs
    Wallace Hall
    Princeton University
    Princeton, New Jersey 08544

Published by the Program in Law and Public Affairs
Produced by the Office of Communications
Printed by the Office of University Printing and Mailing
Princeton University

ISBN 0-9711859-0-5

CONTENTS

Preface by Stephen Macedo   11

Foreword by Hon. Mary Robinson   15

Introduction and Principles   23

Commentary   39

Project Participants   59

Acknowledgments   67

Preface

The Princeton Project began with a visit to Princeton by William J. Butler and Stephen A. Oxman in January 2000. They came, representing the International Commission of Jurists and the American Association for the International Commission of Jurists, to propose the idea of formulating principles to help clarify and bring order to an increasingly important area of international criminal law: prosecutions for serious crimes under international law in national courts based on universal jurisdiction, absent traditional jurisdictional links to the victims or perpetrators of crimes. Dean Michael Rothschild of the Woodrow Wilson School of Public and International Affairs asked me to join the meeting in my capacity as Founding Director of Princeton's new Program in Law and Public Affairs. The idea had great appeal as a chance to bring scholars and jurists together to reflect upon an important problem in the law, and to think about how to address it. Our hope all along has been to wed theory and practice: to study a set of difficult problems of international justice and law with the goal of formulating consensus principles.

The Princeton Project has consisted mainly of various working groups, assembled on the basis of expertise, and with an eye to representing a variety of points of view. Our aim has been to study the problems raised by universal jurisdiction, but also to produce principles in a timely manner. An initial draft of the Principles was produced by Professor M. Cherif Bassiouni. This was discussed at Princeton University on November 10-11, 2000, by a group of leading scholars who also contributed working papers on various aspects of universal jurisdiction. A drafting committee helped redraft the Principles, which were then forwarded along with the revised working papers to an international group of jurists who met at Princeton, January 25-27, 2001.[1]

---

[1] Lists of all official participants can be found below. The collection of papers written for this project is presently under review at Princeton University Press. See below p. 40, note 3.

Preface

The January meeting of the Princeton Project included jurists from around the world who met to hammer out consensus principles. The Princeton Principles, including the introductory matter, emerged in their present form from this meeting, and were re-circulated in February 2001 to Project participants and dozens of human rights organizations around the world, some of whom offered us comments.

We have tried to keep the process of formulating these Principles as open and transparent as possible, while also taking seriously the need to assemble representative and workable groups of participants.

Professor M. Cherif Bassiouni deserves special thanks for his lead role in drafting and revising the principles over the course of many months. His vast expertise and tireless energy have been essential at every stage.

My thanks to the scholars who contributed essential intellectual underpinnings to this Project, and also to the jurists who assembled from around the world in January: their acuity and moral seriousness were all that we could have hoped for and more. Thanks to the many others who provided valuable assistance, including three at Princeton: Professors Gary J. Bass, Richard A. Falk, and Diane Orentlicher (who was here as Fellow, 2000-2001, in the Program in Law and Public Affairs).

Thanks finally to Bill Butler and Steve Oxman for bringing this idea to Princeton University. They furnished me with an unexpected but rewarding inaugural project for the Program in Law and Public Affairs. Steve Oxman's careful attention to matters large and small improved every aspect of this Project. Bill Butler's well-known energy and depth of commitment to justice under law have powered this Project from the start.

These Principles will not, and are not intended to, end the many controversies that surround universal jurisdiction. I do hope that they clarify what universal jurisdiction is, and how its reasonable and responsible exercise by national courts can promote greater justice for victims of serious crimes under international law.

Stephen Macedo
Project Chair
May 2001

Foreword

The subject of universal jurisdiction is of great relevance to all who work for human rights. I regard the search for ways to end impunity in the case of gross violations of human rights as an essential part of the work of my Office, and an essential instrument in the struggle to defend human rights. I welcome the initiative of the Princeton Project and trust that the wide dissemination of these Principles will play a positive role in developing and clarifying the principle of universal jurisdiction.

In my daily work as High Commissioner for Human Rights I see many situations involving gross, and sometimes widespread, human rights abuses for which the perpetrators often go unpunished. Torture, war crimes — including abuses involving gender-based violence — and enforced disappearances are but a few of these crimes. The recent increase in transnational criminal activity, encouraged by globalization and open borders, has added to the challenges we face in fighting against impunity for such abuses. Trafficking of persons, and of women and children specifically, is an issue of particular concern to my Office. These disturbing trends have given me cause to reflect on the possibilities for alternative means of securing justice and accountability.

Two important and complementary means currently exist for the implementation of international criminal jurisdiction: prosecution by international criminal tribunals and the domestic application of the principle of universal jurisdiction. As far as the former is concerned, I am encouraged by the increasing number of states that are signing and ratifying the Statute of the International Criminal Court, and I hope that this permanent Court will soon be a reality. Even before the Court's establishment, the ICC Statute has proved an invaluable tool in the struggle against impunity. The Statute codifies crimes against humanity for the first time in a multilateral treaty, and it enumerates certain acts as war crimes when committed in non-international armed conflicts.

Foreword

Through its cornerstone principle of complementarity, the ICC Statute highlights the fact that international prosecutions alone will never be sufficient to achieve justice and emphasizes the crucial role of national legal systems in bringing an end to impunity. The sad reality is that territorial states often fail to investigate and prosecute serious human rights abuses. The application of universal jurisdiction is therefore a crucial means of justice.

The principle of universal jurisdiction is based on the notion that certain crimes are so harmful to international interests that states are entitled—and even obliged—to bring proceedings against the perpetrator, regardless of the location of the crime or the nationality of the perpetrator or the victim. Human rights abuses widely considered to be subject to universal jurisdiction include genocide, crimes against humanity, war crimes and torture. While the principle of universal jurisdiction has long existed for these crimes, however, it is rapidly evolving as a result of significant recent developments. I applaud the fact that the Princeton Principles acknowledge that this doctrine continues to develop in law and in practice.

One aspect which might be mentioned is the application of universal jurisdiction to other offenses in international law, since this has been raised recently in various fora. The UN Declaration on the Protection of all Persons from Enforced Disappearances, for example, provides for the exercise of universal jurisdiction for alleged acts of forced disappearances, a vision already contained at the regional level in the Inter-American Convention on Forced Disappearance of Persons. The international community is currently also considering a draft international convention on the protection of all persons from enforced disappearance.

Universal jurisdiction was discussed recently at the symposium on the challenge of borderless cyber-crime to international efforts to combat transnational organized crime, held in conjunction with the signing conference for the UN Convention against Transnational Organized Crime in Palermo, Italy. Discussions in treaty negotiations have raised the question of allowing civil jurisdiction for conduct which constitutes an international crime, in the context of the draft Hague Conference on Jurisdiction and Foreign Judgments in Civil and Commercial Matters. These negotiations are of concern to my Office, as they may have important implications regarding the access to courts for victims seeking remedies for human rights violations. The International Court of Justice is also considering issues related to universal jurisdiction in the ongoing case concerning the arrest warrant against the former Minister for Foreign Affairs of the Democratic Republic of Congo by a Belgian investigating judge, who was seeking his provisional detention for alleged serious violations of international humanitarian law.

These developments suggest that new ground is being broken with regard to the application of the principle of universal jurisdiction. This is not to say, however, that the exercise of universal jurisdiction is an easy matter. There are significant practical and legal challenges regarding the application of this principle. The obstacles faced by universal jurisdiction were recently elaborated by the International Law Association in its very informative report on the subject.

Obstacles to the exercise of universal jurisdiction include the question of the application of sovereign immunity defenses. In this regard, the decision of the British House of Lords in the Pinochet case confirming that former heads of state do not enjoy immunity for the crime of torture under UK law was refreshing and, along with other recent cases, has seriously challenged the notion of immunity from criminal liability for crimes under international law committed in an official capacity.

An additional area that I am particularly concerned about is the issue of amnesty laws. I stress that certain gross violations of human rights and international humanitarian law should not be subject to amnesties. When the United Nations faced the question of signing the Sierra Leone Peace Agreement to end atrocities in that country, the UN specified that the amnesty and pardon provisions in Article IX of the agreement would not apply to international crimes of genocide, crimes against humanity, war crimes and other serious violations of international humanitarian law. We must be cautious not to send the wrong message regarding amnesties for serious violations of human

Foreword

rights and international humanitarian law, and I believe that the Princeton Principles correctly express the position that certain crimes are too heinous to go unpunished.

The exercise of universal jurisdiction holds the promise for greater justice for the victims of serious human rights violations around the world. My Office will continue to monitor developments in this rapidly evolving area, including the ongoing efforts of the Princeton Project to strengthen universal jurisdiction as a tool to end impunity. I encourage the wide dissemination of the Princeton Principles on Universal Jurisdiction.

Mary Robinson
United Nations High Commissioner
for Human Rights

THE PRINCETON

PRINCIPLES

ON

UNIVERSAL

JURISDICTION

THE PRINCETON PRINCIPLES
ON UNIVERSAL JUSRISDICTION

Introduction

The Challenge

During the last century millions of human beings perished as a result of genocide, crimes against humanity, war crimes, and other serious crimes under international law. Perpetrators deserving of prosecution have only rarely been held accountable. To stop this cycle of violence and to promote justice, impunity for the commission of serious crimes must yield to accountability. But how can this be done, and what will be the respective roles of national courts and international tribunals?

National courts administer systems of criminal law designed to provide justice for victims and due process for accused persons. A nation's courts exercise jurisdiction over crimes committed in its territory and proceed against those crimes committed abroad by its nationals, or against its nationals, or against its national interests. When these and other connections are absent, national courts may nevertheless exercise jurisdiction under international law over crimes of such exceptional gravity that they affect the fundamental interests of the international community as a whole. This is universal jurisdiction: it is jurisdiction based solely on the nature of the crime. National courts can exercise universal jurisdiction to prosecute and punish, and thereby deter, heinous acts recognized as serious crimes under international law. When national courts exercise universal jurisdiction appropriately, in accordance with internationally recognized standards of due pro-

Introduction to Principles

cess, they act to vindicate not merely their own interests and values but the basic interests and values common to the international community.

Universal jurisdiction holds out the promise of greater justice, but the jurisprudence of universal jurisdiction is disparate, disjointed, and poorly understood. So long as that is so, this weapon against impunity is potentially beset by incoherence, confusion, and, at times, uneven justice.

International criminal tribunals also have a vital role to play in combating impunity as a complement to national courts. In the wake of mass atrocities and of oppressive rule, national judicial systems have often been unable or unwilling to prosecute serious crimes under international law, so international criminal tribunals have been established. Treaties entered into in the aftermath of World War II have strengthened international institutions, and have given greater clarity and force to international criminal law. A signal achievement of this long historic process occurred at a United Nations Conference in July 1998 when the Rome Statute of the International Criminal Court was adopted. When this permanent court becomes effective, the international community will acquire an unprecedented opportunity to hold accountable some of those accused of serious crimes under international law. The jurisdiction of the International Criminal Court will, however, be available only if justice cannot be done at the national level. The primary burden of prosecuting the alleged perpetrators of these crimes will continue to reside with national legal systems.

Enhancing the proper exercise of universal jurisdiction by national courts will help close the gap in law enforcement that has favored perpetrators of serious crimes under international law. Fashioning clearer and sounder principles to guide the exercise of universal jurisdiction by national courts should help to punish, and thereby to deter and prevent, the commission of these heinous crimes. Nevertheless, the aim of sound principles cannot be simply to facilitate the speediest exercise of criminal jurisdiction, always and everywhere, and irrespective of circumstances. Improper exercises of criminal jurisdiction, including universal jurisdiction, may be used merely to harass political

Introduction to Principles

opponents, or for aims extraneous to criminal justice. Moreover, the imprudent or untimely exercise of universal jurisdiction could disrupt the quest for peace and national reconciliation in nations struggling to recover from violent conflict or political oppression. Prudence and good judgment are required here, as elsewhere in politics and law.

What is needed are principles to guide, as well as to give greater coherence and legitimacy to, the exercise of universal jurisdiction. These principles should promote greater accountability for perpetrators of serious crimes under international law, in ways consistent with a prudent concern for the abuse of power and a reasonable solicitude for the quest for peace.

The Princeton Project

The Princeton Project on Universal Jurisdiction has been formed to contribute to the ongoing development of universal jurisdiction. The Project is sponsored by Princeton University's Program in Law and Public Affairs and the Woodrow Wilson School of Public and International Affairs, the International Commission of Jurists, the American Association for the International Commission of Jurists, the Urban Morgan Institute for Human Rights, and the Netherlands Institute of Human Rights. The Project convened at Princeton University in January 2001 an assembly of scholars and jurists from around the world, serving in their personal capacities, to develop consensus principles on universal jurisdiction.*

This assembly of scholars and jurists represented a diversity of viewpoints and a variety of legal systems. They are, however, united in their desire to promote greater legal accountability for those accused of committing serious crimes under international law.

---

* A list of those who assembled in January 2001 can be found below at pp. 59–61.

Introduction to Principles

The Project benefited from the indispensable efforts of leading scholars whom it had commissioned to write working papers on various aspects of universal jurisdiction and who gathered in Princeton in November 2000 to discuss these papers and an early draft of these Principles.*

On January 27, 2001, those assembled at Princeton University to participate in the Princeton Project on Universal Jurisdiction, after considerable and thoughtful debate, arrived at a final text. Each participant might have chosen different words to restate existing international law and to identify the aspirations implicit in international law, but in the end the Principles were adopted.**

The development and adoption of these Principles is part of an ongoing process taking place in different countries and involving scholars, researchers, government experts, international organizations, and other members of international civil society. Those involved in these efforts share the goals of advancing international criminal justice and human rights.

These Principles on Universal Jurisdiction are intended to be useful to legislators seeking to ensure that national laws conform to international law, to judges called upon to interpret and apply international law and to consider whether national law conforms to their state's international legal obligations, to government officials of all kinds exercising their powers under both national and international law, to nongovernmental organizations and members of civil society active in the promotion of international criminal justice and human rights, and to citizens who wish to better understand what international law is and what the international legal order might become.

The assembly is as mindful of the importance of universal jurisdiction as it is of the potential dangers of the abusive or vexatious exercise of criminal jurisdiction, including universal jurisdiction. It has therefore reaffirmed throughout the Principles legal and judicial safeguards

---

*   A list of these scholars can be found below at p. 63.

**   One participant did not join in the adoption, as indicated below at p. 49.

Introduction to Principles

to help deter potential abuses. These safeguards established in international due process norms to protect persons accused of crimes are especially important in the case of a person facing prosecution, based solely on universal jurisdiction, in a state that is not that person's state of nationality or residence.

Furthermore, the assembly recognizes that a scarcity of resources, time, and attention may impose practical limitations on the quest for perfect justice, and that societies emerging from conflict must sometimes allocate priorities among initiatives that contribute to a just and lasting peace, including accountability for international crimes. Moreover, the assembly acknowledges that a range of reasonable disagreement sometimes exists within societies and among societies about the culpability of alleged criminals, the good faith of prosecutions, and the wisdom and practicality of pursuing alleged perpetrators. For these reasons, universal jurisdiction should be exercised with prudence and in a way that ensures the application of the highest standards of prosecutorial fairness and of judicial independence, impartiality, and fairness.

The assembly commends these Principles to states in the belief that their implementation will promote justice, reinforce the rule of law, and advance the other values and goals described above.

The Princeton Principles on Universal Jurisdiction

The participants in the Princeton Project on Universal Jurisdiction propose the following principles for the purposes of advancing the continued evolution of international law and the application of international law in national legal systems:

Principle 1 — Fundamentals of Universal Jurisdiction

1. For purposes of these Principles, universal jurisdiction is criminal jurisdiction based solely on the nature of the crime, without regard to where the crime was committed, the nationality of the alleged or convicted perpetrator, the nationality of the victim, or any other connection to the state exercising such jurisdiction.

2. Universal jurisdiction may be exercised by a competent and ordinary judicial body of any state in order to try a person duly accused of committing serious crimes under international law as specified in Principle 2(1), provided the person is present before such judicial body.

3. A state may rely on universal jurisdiction as a basis for seeking the extradition of a person accused or convicted of committing a serious crime under in-

The Princeton Principles

ternational law as specified in Principle 2(1), provided that it has established a prima facie case of the person's guilt and that the person sought to be extradited will be tried or the punishment carried out in accordance with international norms and standards on the protection of human rights in the context of criminal proceedings.

4. In exercising universal jurisdiction or in relying upon universal jurisdiction as a basis for seeking extradition, a state and its judicial organs shall observe international due process norms including but not limited to those involving the rights of the accused and victims, the fairness of the proceedings, and the independence and impartiality of the judiciary (hereinafter referred to as "international due process norms").

5. A state shall exercise universal jurisdiction in good faith and in accordance with its rights and obligations under international law.

Principle 2 — Serious Crimes Under International Law

1. For purposes of these Principles, serious crimes under international law include: (1) piracy; (2) slavery; (3) war crimes; (4) crimes against peace; (5) crimes against humanity; (6) genocide; and (7) torture.

2. The application of universal jurisdiction to the crimes listed in paragraph 1 is without prejudice to the application of universal jurisdiction to other crimes under international law.

Principle 3 — Reliance on Universal Jurisdiction in the Absence of National Legislation

With respect to serious crimes under international law as specified in Principle 2(1), national judicial organs may rely on universal jurisdiction even if their national legislation does not specifically provide for it.

Principle 4 — Obligation to Support Accountability

1. A state shall comply with all international obligations that are applicable to: prosecuting or extraditing persons accused or convicted of crimes under international law in accordance with a legal process that complies with international due process norms, providing other states investigating or prosecuting such crimes with all available means of administrative and judicial assistance, and undertaking such other necessary and appropriate measures as are consistent with international norms and standards.

2. A state, in the exercise of universal jurisdiction, may, for purposes of prosecution, seek judicial assistance to obtain evidence from another state, provided that the requesting state has a good faith basis and that the evidence sought will be used in accordance with international due process norms.

Principle 5 — Immunities

With respect to serious crimes under international law as specified in Principle 2(1), the official position of any accused person, whether as head of state or government or as a responsible government official, shall not relieve such person of criminal responsibility nor mitigate punishment.

Principle 6 — Statutes of Limitations

Statutes of limitations or other forms of prescription shall not apply to serious crimes under international law as specified in Principle 2(1).

Principle 7 — Amnesties

1. Amnesties are generally inconsistent with the obligation of states to provide accountability for serious crimes under international law as specified in Principle in 2(1).

2. The exercise of universal jurisdiction with respect to serious crimes under international law as specified in Principle 2(1) shall not be precluded by amnesties which are incompatible with the international legal obligations of the granting state.

Principle 8 — Resolution of Competing National Jurisdictions

Where more than one state has or may assert jurisdiction over a person and where the state that has custody of the person has no basis for jurisdiction other than the principle of universality, that state or its judicial organs shall, in deciding whether to prosecute or extradite, base their decision on an aggregate balance of the following criteria:

(a) multilateral or bilateral treaty obligations;

(b) the place of commission of the crime;

(c) the nationality connection of the alleged perpetrator to the requesting state;

(d) the nationality connection of the victim to the requesting state;

(e) any other connection between the requesting state and the alleged perpetrator, the crime, or the victim;

(f) the likelihood, good faith, and effectiveness of the prosecution in the requesting state;

(g) the fairness and impartiality of the proceedings in the requesting state;

(h) convenience to the parties and witnesses, as well as the availability of evidence in the requesting state; and

(i) the interests of justice.

The Princeton Principles

Principle 9 — *Non Bis In Idem*/ Double Jeopardy

1. In the exercise of universal jurisdiction, a state or its judicial organs shall ensure that a person who is subject to criminal proceedings shall not be exposed to multiple prosecutions or punishment for the same criminal conduct where the prior criminal proceedings or other accountability proceedings have been conducted in good faith and in accordance with international norms and standards. Sham prosecutions or derisory punishment resulting from a conviction or other accountability proceedings shall not be recognized as falling within the scope of this Principle.

2. A state shall recognize the validity of a proper exercise of universal jurisdiction by another state and shall recognize the final judgment of a competent and ordinary national judicial body or a competent international judicial body exercising such jurisdiction in accordance with international due process norms.

3. Any person tried or convicted by a state exercising universal jurisdiction for serious crimes under international law as specified in Principle 2(1) shall have the right and legal standing to raise before any national or international judicial body the claim of *non bis in idem* in opposition to any further criminal proceedings.

Principle 10 — Grounds for Refusal of Extradition

1. A state or its judicial organs shall refuse to entertain a request for extradition based on universal jurisdiction if the person sought is likely to face a death penalty sentence or to be subjected to torture or any other cruel, degrading, or inhuman punishment or treatment, or if it is likely that the person sought will be subjected to sham proceedings in which international due process norms will be violated and no satisfactory assurances to the contrary are provided.

2. A state which refuses to extradite on the basis of this Principle shall, when permitted by international law, prosecute the individual accused of a serious crime under international law as specified in Principle 2(1) or extradite such person to another state where this can be done without exposing him or her to the risks referred to in paragraph 1.

Principle 11 — Adoption of National Legislation

A state shall, where necessary, enact national legislation to enable the exercise of universal jurisdiction and the enforcement of these Principles.

Principle 12 — Inclusion of Universal Jurisdiction in Future Treaties

In all future treaties, and in protocols to existing treaties, concerned with serious crimes under international law as specified in Principle 2(1), states shall include provisions for universal jurisdiction.

Principle 13 — Strengthening Accountability and Universal Jurisdiction

1. National judicial organs shall construe national law in a manner that is consistent with these Principles.

2. Nothing in these Principles shall be construed to limit the rights and obligations of a state to prevent or punish, by lawful means recognized under international law, the commission of crimes under international law.

3. These Principles shall not be construed as limiting the continued development of universal jurisdiction in international law.

Principle 14 — Settlement of Disputes

1. Consistent with international law and the Charter of the United Nations states should settle their disputes arising out of the exercise of universal jurisdiction by all available means of peaceful settlement of disputes and in particular by submitting the dispute to the International Court of Justice.

2. Pending the determination of the issue in dispute, a state seeking to exercise universal jurisdiction shall not detain the accused person nor seek to have that person detained by another state unless there is a reasonable risk of flight and no other reasonable means can be found to ensure that person's eventual appearance before the judicial organs of the state seeking to exercise its jurisdiction.

Commentary on the Princeton Principles [1]

Why principles? Why now?

The Princeton Principles on Universal Jurisdiction (Principles) are a progressive restatement of international law on the subject of universal jurisdiction. Leading scholars and jurists gathered twice at Princeton University to help clarify this important area of law.[2] The Principles contain elements of both *lex lata* (the law as it is) and *de lege ferenda* (the law as it ought to be), but they should not be understood to limit the future evolution of universal jurisdiction. The Principles are intended to help guide national legislative bodies seeking to enact implementing legislation; judges who may be required to construe universal jurisdiction in applying domestic law or in making extradition decisions; governments that must decide whether to prosecute or extradite, or otherwise to assist in promoting international criminal accountability; and all those in civil society concerned with bringing to justice perpetrators of serious international crimes.

Participants in the Princeton Project discussed several difficult threshold questions concerning universal jurisdiction. How firmly is universal jurisdiction established in international law? It is of course recognized in treaties, national legislation, judicial opinions, and the

---

[1] Prepared by Steven W. Becker (J.D., DePaul University College of Law, June 2001), Sullivan Fellow, International Human Rights Law Institute. This Commentary was prepared under the direction of Professor M. Cherif Bassiouni and with the assistance of Stephen Macedo, Stephen A. Oxman, and others.

[2] The first meeting, in November 2000, was attended by leading academics who wrote and discussed scholarly papers on various aspects of universal jurisdiction. The assembly at the second meeting, in January 2001, was composed of distinguished legal scholars including some of the academics who attended the first meeting. Lists of attendees follow this Commentary.

Commentary

writings of scholars, but not everyone draws the same conclusions from these sources. Commentators even disagree on how to ascertain whether universal jurisdiction is well established in customary international law: for some, the acceptance by states that a practice is obligatory *(opinio juris)* is enough; for others, the consistent practice of states is required.

When it is agreed that an obligation has been created in a treaty, legal systems differ in how they incorporate international obligations into domestic law. In many legal systems, the national judiciary cannot apply universal jurisdiction in the absence of national legislation. In other systems it is possible for the judiciary to rely directly on treaties and customary international law without waiting for implementing legislation. (These and other complexities will be explored in a collection of essays being published under the auspices of the Princeton Project.[3]) Accordingly, Principle 3 encourages courts to rely on universal jurisdiction in the absence of national legislation, so long as their legal systems permit them to do so. Principle 11 calls upon legislatures to enact laws enabling the exercise of universal jurisdiction. Principle 12 calls for states to provide for universal jurisdiction in future treaties and protocols to existing treaties.

Participants in the Princeton Project also carefully considered whether the time is ripe to bring greater clarity to universal jurisdiction. While it has been with us for centuries, universal jurisdiction seems only now to be coming into its own as a systematic means for promoting legal accountability. Universal jurisdiction was given

---

[3] This collection, being edited by Stephen Macedo, is under review at Princeton University Press. It will include: M. Cherif Bassiouni, *Universal Jurisdiction in Historical Perspective;* Georges Abi-Saab, *Universal Jurisdiction and International Criminal Tribunals: A Study of Interaction;* Gary J. Bass, *The Adolph Eichmann Case;* Richard A. Falk, *Assessing the Pinochet Litigation: Whither Universal Jurisdiction?;* Stephen P. Marks, *The Hissène Habré Case: The Law and Politics of Universal Jurisdiction;* Chandra Lekha Sriram & Jordan J. Paust, *Universal Jurisdiction and Responsibility: A Survey of Current, Impending, and Potential Cases;* Hon. Justice Michael Kirby, *Universal Jurisdiction and Judicial Reluctance: A New "Fourteen Points";* Leila Nadya Sadat, *Universal Jurisdiction and National Amnesties, Truth Commissions and Other Alternatives to Prosecution: Giving Justice a Chance;* Anne-Marie Slaughter, *The Limits of Universal Jurisdiction;* Diane F. Orentlicher, *Frontiers of Universal Jurisdiction;* A. Hays Butler, *A Survey of Enabling Statutes.*

Commentary

great prominence by the proceedings in London involving former Chilean leader General Augusto Pinochet, and now courts around the world are seriously considering indictments involving universal jurisdiction.[4]

In light of current dynamics in international criminal law, some supporters of universal jurisdiction question whether now is the time to clarify the principles that should guide its exercise. Might it not be better to wait to allow for unpredictable, and perhaps surprisingly progressive, developments? Is there a danger of stunting the development of universal jurisdiction by articulating guiding principles prematurely?

Everyone connected with the Princeton Project took this problem seriously. It commonly arises when codification is undertaken. Nevertheless, these concerns seem especially significant in the case of universal jurisdiction, given the wide gulf between what the law of universal jurisdiction is and what advocates of greater justice would like it to be.

After considerable discussion, those who gathered in Princeton in January 2001 favored our effort to bring greater clarity and order to the use of universal jurisdiction. Our aim is to help guide those who believe that national courts have a vital role to play in combating impunity even when traditional jurisdictional connections are absent. These Principles should help clarify the legal bases for the responsible and reasoned exercise of universal jurisdiction. Insofar as universal jurisdiction is exercised, and seen to be exercised, in a reasoned, lawful, and orderly manner, it will gain wider acceptance. Mindful of the need to encourage continued progress in international law, these Principles have been drafted so as to invite rather than hinder the continued development of universal jurisdiction.

The Principles are written so as to both clarify the current law of universal jurisdiction and encourage its further development. As already noted, the Principles are addressed sometimes to the legislative, executive, or judicial branches of government, and sometimes to a

---

[4] See Falk, *supra* note 3.

Commentary

combination of these.[5] The Principles are intended for a variety of actors in divergent legal systems who will properly draw on them in different ways. We acknowledge, for example, that in some legal systems, and according to some legal theories, judges are constrained in their ability to interpret existing law in light of aspirations to greater justice, or other principled aims.[6] Nevertheless, judges on international and regional tribunals, and judges on national constitutional and supreme courts, often have greater interpretive latitude. Our hope is that these Principles might inform and shape the practice of those judges and other officials who can act to promote greater justice and legal accountability consistent with the constraints of their offices. We also offer these Principles to help guide and inform citizens, leaders of organizations in civil society, and public officials of all sorts: all of these different actors could benefit from a clearer common understanding of what universal jurisdiction is and when and how it may reasonably be exercised.

When and how to prosecute based on universality?

In defining universal jurisdiction, participants focused on the case of "pure" universal jurisdiction, namely, where the nature of the crime is the sole basis for subject matter jurisdiction. There has been some scholarly confusion on the role of universal jurisdiction in famous prosecutions, such as the trial in Jerusalem of Adolph Eichmann.[7] In addition, it is important to recall that simply because certain offenses are

---

[5] *See, e.g.,* Principle 3 which encourages judicial organs to rely on universal jurisdiction, Principle 11 which calls upon legislatures to enact laws enabling the exercise of universal jurisdiction, and Principle 12 which exhorts governments to include provisions for universal jurisdiction in new treaties and protocols to existing treaties.

[6] *See* Kirby, *supra* note 3.

[7] *See Attorney General of Israel v. Eichmann,* 36 I.L.R. 5 (Isr. D.C., Jerusalem, 12 Dec. 1961), aff'd, 36 I.L.R. 277 (Isr. S. Ct., 29 May 1962), which is often cited as representing the exercise of universal jurisdiction by Israel, although many argue that the decision was more fundamentally predicated upon the passive personality doctrine and the protective principle under a unique Israeli statute passed by the Knesset in 1950. See Bass, supra note 3.

Commentary

universally condemned does not mean that a state may exercise universal jurisdiction over them.

Participants in the Princeton Project debated whether states should in general be encouraged to exercise universal jurisdiction based solely on the seriousness of the alleged crime, without traditional connecting links to the victims or perpetrators of serious crimes under international law. On the one hand, the whole point of universal jurisdiction would seem to be to permit or even encourage prosecution when states find within their territory a non-citizen accused of serious crimes under international law. In this way, universal jurisdiction maximizes accountability and minimizes impunity. The very essence of universal jurisdiction would seem, therefore, to be that national courts should prosecute alleged criminals absent any connecting factors (for example, even if the crimes were not committed against the enforcing states' citizens, or by its citizens).

There is, nevertheless, great concern that particular states will abuse universal jurisdiction to pursue politically motivated prosecutions. Mercenary governments and rogue prosecutors could seek to indict the heads of state or other senior public officials in countries with which they have political disagreements. Powerful states may try to exempt their own leaders from accountability while seeking to prosecute others, defying the basic proposition that equals should be treated equally. Members of peacekeeping forces might be harassed with unjustified prosecutions, and this might deter peacekeeping operations.

Should the Principles insist at least that the accused is physically present in the territory of the enforcing state? Should other connecting links also be required? Participants decided not to include an explicit requirement of a territorial link in Principle 1(1)'s definition. This was done partly to allow for further discussion, partly to avoid stifling the evolution of universal jurisdiction, and partly out of deference to pending litigation in the International Court of Justice.[8] Nevertheless,

---

[8] *See* the International Court of Justice's order in the case of *Arrest Warrant of 11 April 2000* (Congo v. Belg.) (Dec. 8, 2000), in which these issues feature prominently. In a recent development, on March 20, 2001, the Senegalese Cour de Cassation held that Hissène Habré, the former president of Chad, could not be tried on torture charges in Senegal. *See* Marks, *supra* note 3.

Commentary

subsection (2) of Principle 1 holds that a "competent and ordinary" judicial body may try accused persons on the basis of universal jurisdiction "provided the person is present before such judicial body." The language of Principle 1(2) does not prevent a state from initiating the criminal process, conducting an investigation, issuing an indictment, or requesting extradition, when the accused is not present.

The Principles contain a number of provisions describing the standards that legal systems and particular prosecutions would have to meet in order to exercise universal jurisdiction responsibly and legitimately. Subsections (3) and (4) of Principle 1 insist that a state may seek to extradite persons accused or convicted on the basis of universal jurisdiction "provided that it has established a *prima facie* case of the person's guilt" and provided that trials and punishments will take place in accordance with "international due process norms," relevant human rights standards, and the independence and impartiality of the judiciary. Later Principles contain additional safeguards against prosecutorial abuses: Principle 9, for example, guards against repeated prosecutions for the same crime in violation of the principle of *non bis in idem,* or the prohibition on double jeopardy.[9] Principle 10 allows states to refuse requests for extradition if the person sought "is likely to face a death penalty sentence or to be subjected to torture" or cruel or inhuman treatment or sham proceedings in violation of international due process norms. The Principles reinforce proper legal standards for courts and should help guide executive officers considering extradition requests.

Of course, effective legal processes require the active cooperation of different government agencies, including courts and prosecutors. The establishment of international networks of cooperation will be especially important to the effective development of universal jurisdiction.

---

[9] *See* Principle 9. Note also that the drafters intended the international due process norms in Principle 1(4) to be illustrative and not exhaustive. The right to reasonable bail (Cf. Principle 14(2)) and the right to counsel were also referred to as being included among the essential due process guarantees. *See also* Universal Declaration of Human Rights, 10 Dec. 1948, arts. 10, 11, G.A. Res. 217A (III), U.N. Doc. A/810 (1948); International Covenant on Civil and Political Rights, 19 Dec. 1966, arts. 14, 15, 999 U.N.T.S. 171 [hereinafter ICCPR].

Commentary

Therefore, Principle 4 calls upon states to comply with their international obligations to either prosecute or extradite those accused or convicted of crimes under international law, so long as these legal processes comply with "international due process norms." Universal jurisdiction can only work if different states provide each other with active judicial and prosecutorial assistance, and all participating states will need to insure that due process norms are being complied with.

All legal powers can be abused by willfully malicious individuals. The Princeton Principles do all that principles can do to guard against such abuses: they specify the considerations that conscientious international actors can and should act upon.

Which crimes are covered?

The choice of which crimes to include as "serious crimes under international law" was discussed at length in Princeton.[10] The ordering of the list of "serious crimes" was settled by historical progression rather than an attempt to rank crimes based upon their gravity.

- "Piracy" is a crime that paradigmatically is subject to prosecution by any nation based on principles of universality, and it is crucial to the origins of universal jurisdiction, so it comes first.[11]
- "Slavery" was included in part because its historical ties to piracy reach back to the Declaration of the Congress of Vienna in 1815. There are but a few conventional provisions, however,

---

[10] *See* Principle 2(1).

[11] *See, e.g.,* Convention on the High Seas, 29 Apr. 1958, art. 19, 450 U.N.T.S. 82, 13 U.S.T. 2312 ("On the high seas, or in any other place outside the jurisdiction of any state, every state may seize a pirate ship or aircraft, or a ship taken by piracy and under the control of pirates, and arrest the persons and seize the property on board."); United Nations Convention on the Law of the Sea, 10 Dec. 1982, art. 105, U.N. A/CONF.62/122, 21 I.L.M. 1261. *See also* Bassiouni, *supra* note 3.

Commentary

authorizing the exercise of universal jurisdiction for slavery and slave-related practices.[12] The phrase "slavery and slave-related practices" was considered but rejected by the Princeton Assembly as being too technical in nature. However, it was agreed that the term "slavery" was intended to include those practices prohibited in the Supplementary Convention on the Abolition of Slavery, the Slave Trade, and Institutions and Practices Similar to Slavery.[13]

- "War crimes" were initially restricted to "serious war crimes," namely, "grave breaches" of the 1949 Geneva Conventions and Protocol I, in order to avoid the potential for numerous prosecutions based upon less serious violations.[14] The participants, however, did not want to give the impression that some war crimes are not serious, and thus opted not to include the word "serious." The assembly agreed, though, that it would be inappropriate to invoke universal jurisdiction for the prosecution of minor transgressions of the 1949 Geneva Conventions and Protocol I.

---

[12] *Cf.* Convention for the Suppression of the Traffic in Persons and of the Exploitation of the Prostitution of Others, 21 Mar. 1950, art. 11, 96 U.N.T.S. 271 ("Nothing in the present Convention shall be interpreted as determining the attitude of a Party towards the general question of the limits of criminal jurisdiction under international law."); Convention Relative to the Slave Trade and Importation into Africa of Firearms, Ammunition, and Spiritous Liquors, 2 July 1890, art. 5, 27 Stat. 886, 17 Martens Nouveau Recueil (ser. 2) 345; Treaty for the Suppression of the African Slave Trade, 20 Dec. 1841, arts. 6, 7, 10, and annex B, pt. 5, 2 Martens Nouveau Recueil (ser. 1) 392.

[13] 7 Sept. 1956, 266 U.N.T.S. 3, 18 U.S.T. 3201.

[14] *See* Geneva Convention for the Amelioration of the Condition of the Wounded and Sick in Armed Forces in the Field, 12 Aug. 1949, art. 50, 75 U.N.T.S. 31, 6 U.S.T. 3114, T.I.A.S. No. 3362; Geneva Convention for the Amelioration of the Condition of Wounded, Sick and Shipwrecked Members of Armed Forces at Sea, 12 Aug. 1949, art. 51, 75 U.N.T.S. 85, 6 U.S.T. 3217, T.I.A.S. No. 3363; Geneva Convention Relative to the Treatment of Prisoners of War, 12 Aug. 1949, art. 130, 75 U.N.T.S. 135, 6 U.S.T. No. 3316, T.I.A.S. No. 3364; Geneva Convention Relative to the Protection of Civilian Persons in Time of War, 12 Aug. 1949, art. 147, 75 U.N.T.S. 287, 6 U.S.T. 3516, T.I.A.S. No. 3365; Protocol I Additional to the Geneva Conventions of 12 August 1949, 12 Dec. 1977, art. 85, U.N. Doc. A/32/144, Annex I.

- "Crimes against peace" were also discussed at length. While many argue that aggression constitutes the most serious international crime, others contend that defining the crime of "aggression" is in practice extremely difficult and divisive. In the end, "crimes against peace" were included, despite some disagreement, in part in order to recall the wording of Article 6(a) of the Nuremberg Charter.[15]
- "Crimes against humanity" were included without objection, and these crimes have now been authoritatively defined by Article 7 of the Rome Statute of the International Criminal Court.[16] There is not presently any conventional law that provides for the exercise of universal jurisdiction over crimes against humanity.
- "Genocide" was included without objection. Article 6 of the Genocide Convention provides that a person accused of genocide shall be tried in a court of "the State in the territory of which the act was committed."[17] However, Article 6 does not preclude the use of universal jurisdiction by an international penal tribunal, in the event that such a tribunal is established.
- "Torture" was included without objection though some noted that there are some disagreements as to what constitutes torture. "Torture" is intended to include the "other cruel, inhuman, or degrading treatment or punishment" as defined in the Convention Against Torture and Other Cruel, Inhuman or

---

[15] *See* Charter of the International Military Tribunal, 8 Aug. 1945, art. 6(a), 82 U.N.T.S. 284, 59 Stat. 1546 [hereinafter Nuremberg Charter], *annexed to* Agreement for the Prosecution and Punishment of the Major War Criminals of the European Axis, 8 Aug. 1945, 82 U.N.T.S. 279, 59 Stat. 1544.

[16] 17 July 1998, art. 7, U.N. Doc. A/CONF.183/9, 37 I.L.M. 999 [hereinafter ICC Statute].

[17] Convention on the Prevention and Punishment of the Crime of Genocide, 9 Dec. 1948, art. 6, 78 U.N.T.S. 277.

Commentary

Degrading Treatment or Punishment.[18] Moreover, the Torture Convention implicitly provides for the exercise of universal jurisdiction over prohibited conduct.[19]

Apartheid, terrorism, and drug crimes were raised as candidates for inclusion. It should be carefully noted that the list of serious crimes is explicitly illustrative, not exhaustive. Principle 2(1) leaves open the possibility that, in the future, other crimes may be deemed of such a heinous nature as to warrant the application of universal jurisdiction.

When and against whom should universal jurisdiction be exercised?

Among the most difficult questions discussed in the Princeton Project was the enforcement of universal jurisdiction, and the question of when if ever to honor immunities and amnesties with respect to the commission of serious crimes under international law. Especially difficult moral, political, and legal issues surround immunities for former or current heads of state, diplomats, and other officials (see Principle 5). Immunity from international criminal prosecution for sitting heads of state is established by customary international law, and immunity for diplomats is established by treaty. There is an extremely important distinction, however, between "substantive" and "procedural" immunity. A substantive immunity from prosecution would provide heads of state, diplomats, and other officials with exoneration from criminal responsibility for the commission of serious crimes under international law when these crimes are committed in an official capacity. Principle 5 rejects this substantive immunity ("the official position of any accused

---

[18] G.A. Res. 39/46, Annex, U.N. GAOR, 39th Sess., Supp. No. 51, U.N. Doc. A/39/51 (1984), *entered into force* 26 June 1987 [hereinafter Torture Convention], draft reprinted in 23 I.L.M. 1027, modified 24 I.L.M. 535.

[19] *Id.* arts. 5, 7(1).

Commentary

person, whether as head of state or government or as a responsible government official, shall not relieve such person of criminal responsibility nor mitigate punishment"). Nevertheless, in proceedings before national tribunals, procedural immunity remains in effect during a head of state's or other official's tenure in office, or during the period in which a diplomat is accredited to a host state. Under international law as it exists, sitting heads of state, accredited diplomats, and other officials cannot be prosecuted while in office for acts committed in their official capacities.[20]

The Princeton Principles' rejection of substantive immunity keeps faith with the Nuremberg Charter, which proclaims: "The official position of defendants, whether as Heads of State or responsible officials in Government Departments, shall not be considered as freeing them from responsibility or mitigating punishment."[21] More recently, the Statutes of the International Criminal Tribunal for the Former Yugoslavia (ICTY) and that of the International Criminal Tribunal for Rwanda (ICTR) removed substantive immunity for war crimes, genocide, and

---

[20] Lord Browne-Wilkinson provided the following reasons for his dissent from the Princeton Principles:

I am strongly in favour of universal jurisdiction over serious international crimes if, by those words, one means the exercise by an international court or by the courts of one state of jurisdiction over the nationals of another state with the prior consent of that latter state, i.e. in cases such as the ICC and Torture Convention.

But the Princeton Principles propose that individual national courts should exercise such jurisdiction against nationals of a state which has not agreed to such jurisdiction. Moreover the Principles do not recognize any form of sovereign immunity: Principle 5(1). If the law were to be so established, states antipathetic to Western powers would be likely to seize both active and retired officials and military personnel of such Western powers and stage a show trial for alleged international crimes. Conversely, zealots in Western States might launch prosecutions against, for example, Islamic extremists for their terrorist activities. It is naïve to think that, in such cases, the national state of the accused would stand by and watch the trial proceed: resort to force would be more probable. In any event the fear of such legal actions would inhibit the use of peacekeeping forces when it is otherwise desirable and also the free interchange of diplomatic personnel.

I believe that the adoption of such universal jurisdiction without preserving the existing concepts of immunity would be more likely to damage than to advance chances of international peace.

[21] Nuremberg Charter, *supra* note 15, art. 7.

Commentary

crimes against humanity.[22] Principle 5 in fact tracks the language of these statutes, which, in turn, were fashioned from Article 7 of the Nuremberg Charter.[23]

None of these statutes addresses the issue of procedural immunity. Customary international law, however, is quite clear on the subject: heads of state enjoy unqualified "act of state" immunity during their term of office. Similarly, diplomats accredited to a host state enjoy unqualified *ex officio* immunity during the performance

---

[22] *See* Statute of the International Criminal Tribunal for the Former Yugoslavia, art. 7(2), S.C. Res. 808, U.N. SCOR, 48th Sess., 3175th mtg., U.N. Doc. S/RES/808 (1993), *annexed to Report of the Secretary-General pursuant to Paragraph 2 of U.N. Security Council Resolution 808* (1993), U.N. Doc. S/25704 & Add.1 (1993) [hereinafter ICTY Statute]; Statute of the International Criminal Tribunal for Rwanda, art. 6(2), S.C. Res. 955, U.N. SCOR, 49th Sess., 3453d mtg., Annex, U.N. Doc. S/RES/955 (1994) [hereinafter ICTR Statute].

[23] *See* ICTY Statute, *supra* note 22, art. 7(2); ICTR Statute, *supra* note 22, art. 6(2). Article 27 of the ICC Statute similarly provides:
   1. This Statute shall apply equally to all persons without any distinction based on official capacity. In particular, official capacity as a Head of State or Government, a member of a Government or parliament, an elected representative or a government official shall in no case exempt a person from criminal responsibility under this Statute, nor shall it, in and of itself, constitute a ground for reduction of sentence.
   2. Immunities or special procedural rules which may attach to the official capacity of a person, whether under national or international law, shall not bar the Court from exercising its jurisdiction over such a person.

   ICC Statute, *supra* note 16, art. 27.
   Article 98 of the ICC Statute, however, yields to the primacy of other multilateral treaties in assessing immunity:
   1. The Court may not proceed with a request for surrender or assistance which would require the requested State to act inconsistently with its obligations under international law with respect to the State or diplomatic immunity of a person or property of a third State, unless the Court can first obtain the cooperation of that third State for the waiver of the immunity.
   2. The Court may not proceed with a request for surrender which would require the requested State to act inconsistently with its obligations under international agreements pursuant to which the consent of a sending State is required to surrender a person of that State to the Court, unless the Court can first obtain the cooperation of the sending State for the giving of consent for the surrender.

   Id. art. 98.
   Note that Article 27 is located in Part III of the ICC Statute; while Article 98 is contained in Part IX of the Statute, which contains no prohibitions on immunities, and thus seems to permit a head of state, diplomat, or other official to invoke procedural immunity, where applicable.

of their official duties.[24] A head of state, diplomat, or other official may, therefore, be immune from prosecution while in office, but once they step down any claim of immunity becomes ineffective, and they are then subject to the possibility of prosecution.

The Principles do not purport to revoke the protections afforded by procedural immunity, but neither do they affirm procedural immunities as a matter of principle. In the future, procedural immunities for sitting heads of state, diplomats, and other officials may be called increasingly into question, a possibility prefigured by the ICTY's indictment of Slobodan Milošević while still a sitting head of state.[25] Whether this unprecedented action will become the source of a new regime in international law remains to be seen. Participants in the Princeton Project opted not to try and settle on principles governing procedural immunity in order to leave space for future developments.

Another possible limit on the prosecution of "serious crimes under international law" are statutes of limitations.[26] Principle 6 reaffirms that statutes of limitations do not apply to crimes covered by universal jurisdiction. Conventional international law supports this position, at least as concerns war crimes and crimes against humanity.[27] Admittedly, the practice of states leaves something to be desired, here as elsewhere. Subsection (1) of Principle 13 provides that national judicial organs shall construe their own law in a manner "consis-

---

[24] *See* Vienna Convention on Diplomatic Relations, 18 Apr. 1961, 500 U.N.T.S. 95, 23 U.S.T. 3227; *see also* United States Diplomatic and Consular Staff in Tehran (U.S. v. Iran), 1980 I.C.J. 3 (May 24). These temporary immunities are not revoked by this subsection. Such doctrines, however, may be in the process of erosion. *See infra* note 25 and accompanying text.

[25] Prosecutor v. Milošević (Indictment) (24 May 1999), *at* http://www.un.org/icty/indictment/english/mil-ii990524e.htm.

[26] *See* Principle 6.

[27] *See* Convention on the Non-Applicability of Statutory Limitations to War Crimes and Crimes Against Humanity, 26 Nov. 1968, 754 U.N.T.S. 73; European Convention on Non-Applicability of Statutory Limitations to Crimes Against Humanity and War Crimes (Inter-European), 25 Jan. 1974, Europ. T.S. No. 82.

Commentary

tent with these Principles." If a nation's law is silent as to a limitations period with respect to a certain serious crime under international law, for example genocide, a local judge could draw on this subsection and legitimately *refuse* to apply by analogy another statute of limitations for a crime that was codified, *e.g.,* murder. Because the laws of many nations include limitations periods, a number of participants suggested that the Principles should exhort states to eliminate statutes of limitations for serious crimes under international law; Principle 11 does this.

Another significant discussion took place on the topics of amnesties and other pardons that might be granted by a state or by virtue of a treaty to individuals or categories of individuals. Some participants were very strongly against the inclusion of any principle that recognized an amnesty for "serious crimes under international law." Others felt that certain types of amnesties, coupled with accountability mechanisms other than criminal prosecution, were acceptable in some cases: at least in difficult periods of political transition, as a second best alternative to criminal prosecution. Much controversy surrounds accountability mechanisms such as South Africa's Truth and Reconciliation Commission. We considered trying to specify the minimum prerequisites that should have to be satisfied in order for accountability mechanisms to be deemed legitimate (including such features as individualized accountability), but in the end those assembled at Princeton decided not to try and provide general criteria. Accordingly, Principle 7 expresses only a presumption that amnesties are inconsistent with a state's obligations to prevent impunity.[28] Subsection (2) recognizes that if a state grants amnesties that are inconsistent with obligations to hold perpetrators of serious international crimes accountable, other states may still seek to exercise universal jurisdiction.

---

[28] *See* Principle 7(1).

Commentary

Who should prosecute?

Principle 8 seeks to specify factors that should be considered when making judgments about whether to prosecute or extradite in the face of competing national claims. The list of factors is not intended to be exhaustive.[29] This Principle is designed to provide states with guidelines for the resolution of conflicts in situations in which the state with custody over a person accused of serious international crimes can base its jurisdiction solely on universality, and one or more other states have asserted or are in a position to exercise jurisdiction.

Originally, the drafters expressed a preference for ranking the different bases of jurisdiction so as to indicate which should receive priority in the case of a conflict. Almost without exception, the territorial principle was thought to deserve precedence. This was in part because of the longstanding conviction that a criminal defendant should be tried by his "natural judge." Many participants expressed the view that societies that have been victimized by political crimes should have the opportunity to bring the perpetrators to justice, provided their judiciaries are able and willing to do so.

Although it was decided not to rank jurisdictional claims, the Principles do not deny that some traditional jurisdictional claims will often be especially weighty. For example, the exercise of territorial jurisdiction will often also satisfy several of the other factors enumerated in Principle 8, such as the convenience to the parties and witnesses, as well as the availability of evidence.

---

[29] This method of listing relevant factors has been employed in other similar contexts, such as in determining jurisdictional priority over extraterritorial crime, *see* RESTATEMENT (THIRD) OF FOREIGN RELATIONS LAW OF THE UNITED STATES § 403 (1987), and in resolving conflict of laws problems, *see* RESTATEMENT (SECOND) OF CONFLICT OF LAWS § 6 (1971).

Commentary

What protections for the accused?

If universal jurisdiction is to be a tool for promoting greater justice, the rights of the accused must be protected. Principle 9 protects accused persons against multiple prosecutions for the same crime. There was no objection among the participants as to desirability of such safeguards. Several of the participants, however, questioned whether the prohibition on double jeopardy—*non bis in idem*—was a recognized principle of international law. Under regional human rights agreements, *non bis in idem* has been interpreted to apply within a state, but not between states. It was noted, however, that the importance of the doctrine of *non bis in idem* is recognized in almost all legal systems: it qualifies as a general principle of law and, as such, could be said to apply under international law.[30] Subsection (3) specifically grants an accused the right "and legal standing" to invoke the claim of *non bis in idem* as a defense to further criminal proceedings. This provision is designed to allow a defendant to independently raise this defense in jurisdictions that would otherwise only permit the requested state, in its discretion, to invoke the double jeopardy principle on an accused person's behalf.

Subsection (1) of Principle 10 requires that an extradition request predicated upon universality be refused if the accused is likely to face the death penalty, torture, or "other cruel, degrading, or inhuman punishment or treatment." This latter phraseology should be construed in accord with its usage as described in the Torture Convention.[31]

There was also some discussion about whether to include a provision on trials *in absentia* in the Principles. Although generally considered anathema in common law countries, such trials are traditional in certain civil law nations, such as France, and serve a valuable function with respect to the preservation of evidence. In the end it was decided not to refer to such trials in the Principles.

---

[30] It is also included in the ICCPR, *supra* note 9, art. 14(7), and the American Convention on Human Rights, 22 Nov. 1969, art. 8(4), 1144 U.N.T.S. 123, O.A.S. T.S. No. 36.

[31] *See* Torture Convention, *supra* note 18, art. 1.

Commentary

Conclusion: Promoting accountability through international law

Several of the remaining principles have already been mentioned, and their import should be clear. Principles 11 and 12 call upon states both to adopt legislation to enable the exercise of universal jurisdiction and to include provisions for universal jurisdiction in all future treaties. The first sentence of Principle 13 was included by the drafters to memorialize their intention that nothing in the Principles should be construed as altering the existing obligations of any state under terrorism conventions.

Subsection (1) of Principle 14 calls for states to peacefully settle disputes arising out of the application of universal jurisdiction. An example of the appropriate resolution sought by this subsection is the case of *Democratic Republic of the Congo v. Belgium*, which is pending before the International Court of Justice as these Principles go to press.[32] The case involves a dispute regarding Belgium's assetion of universal jurisdiction over the Congo's Minister of Foreign Affairs.

Universal jurisdiction is one means to achieve accountability and to deny impunity to those accused of serious international crimes. It reflects the maxim embedded in so many treaties: *aut dedere aut judicare,* the duty to extradite or prosecute. All of the participants in the Princeton Project felt it important that the Principles not be construed to limit the development of universal jurisdiction or to constrain the evolution of accountability for crimes under international law, and this conviction is made explicit in Principle 13.

National courts exercising universal jurisdiction have a vital role to play in bringing perpetrators of international crimes to justice: they form part of the web of legal instruments which can and should be deployed to combat impunity. The Princeton Principles do not purport to define the proper use of universal jurisdiction in any final way. Our hope is that these Principles can bring greater clarity and order to the exercise of universal jurisdiction, and thereby encourage its reasonable and responsible use.

---

[32] *Arrest Warrant of 11 April 2000* (Congo v. Belg.) (Dec. 8, 2000).

Project Participants, Adoption of Principles, January 25-27, 2001

Adrian Arena
Acting Secretary General
International Commission of Jurists

Lloyd Axworthy
Director of the Liu Centre for the Study of Global Issues, University of British Columbia; Former Minister of Foreign Affairs of the Federal Government of Canada

Gary J. Bass
Assistant Professor of Politics and International Affairs, Princeton University

M. Cherif Bassiouni
Professor of Law and President of the International Human Rights Law Institute, DePaul College of Law

Nicolas Browne-Wilkinson *
Law Lord, House of Lords of the United Kingdom

* Did not join in the adoption. See *infra* at p. 49, note 20.

William J. Butler
Former Chairman of the Executive Committee of the International Commission of Jurists 1975-1990; President of the American Association for the International Commission of Jurists

Hans Corell
Under-Secretary-General for Legal Affairs, United Nations

Param Cumaraswamy
United Nations Special Rapporteur on the Independence of the Judiciary, United Nations

E.V.O. Dankwa
Professor of Law, University of Ghana
Chair, African Commission on Human and Peoples Rights

Richard A. Falk
Albert G. Milbank Professor of International Law and Practice, Professor of Politics and International Affairs, Princeton University

Participants

Tom Farer
Dean of the Graduate School of International Studies, University of Denver

Cees Flinterman
Professor of Human Rights, Utrecht University; Director of the Netherlands Institute of Human Rights and the Netherlands School of Human Rights Research

Mingxuan Gao
Professor of Law, China Law Institute

Menno T. Kamminga
Professor of Public International Law, Maastricht University

Michael Kirby
Justice, High Court of Australia

Bert B. Lockwood
Distinguished Service Professor of Law; Director of the Urban Morgan Institute for Human Rights, University of Cincinnati College of Law

Stephen Macedo
Laurance S. Rockefeller Professor of Politics and the University Center for Human Values; Director of the Program in Law and Public Affairs, Princeton University

Stephen P. Marks
François Xavier Bagnoud Professor, Harvard School of Public Health

Michael O'Boyle
Section Registrar, European Court of Human Rights

Diane F. Orentlicher
Law and Public Affairs Fellow, 2000-2001, Princeton University; Professor of Law and Director of the War Crimes Research Office, American University

Stephen A. Oxman
Member of the Board of Directors, American Association for the International Commission of Jurists, and Former U.S. Assistant Secretary of State for European and Canadian Affairs

Vesselin Popovski
Professor of Law, University of Exeter

Michael Posner
Executive Director, Lawyers Committee for Human Rights

Yves Sandoz
Former Director of Principles and International Law, International Committee of the Red Cross

Participants

Jerome J. Shestack
Former President, American Bar Association; Member of the Executive Committee, International Commission of Jurists

Stephen M. Schwebel
Former President, International Court of Justice

Kuniji Shibahara
Professor Emeritus, University of Tokyo

Anne-Marie Slaughter
J. Sinclair Armstrong Professor of International, Foreign and Comparative Law; Director of Graduate and International Legal Studies, Harvard Law School

Turgut Tarhanli
Professor of International Law, Istanbul Bilgi University

Wang Xiumei
Senior Researcher, Renmin University of China

Attendees, Meeting of Scholars, November 10-11, 2000

Georges Abi-Saab
Professor of International Law, The Graduate Institute of International Studies

Gary J. Bass
Assistant Professor of Politics and International Affairs, Princeton University

M. Cherif Bassiouni
Professor of Law and President of the International Human Rights Law Institute, DePaul University College of Law

George A. Bermann
Charles Keller Beekman Professor of Law and Director of the European Legal Studies Center, Columbia Law School

William J. Butler
Former Chairman of the Executive Committee of the International Commission of Jurists, 1975-1990, and President of the American Association for the International Commission of Jurists

Lori F. Damrosch
Henry L. Moses Professor of International Law and Organization, Columbia Law School

Pablo De Greiff
Assistant Professor of Philosophy at the State University of New York at Buffalo, Laurance S. Rockefeller Visiting Fellow, 2000-2001, Princeton University Center for Human Values

Richard A. Falk
Albert G. Milbank Professor of International Law and Practice, and Professor of Politics and International Affairs, Princeton University

Cees Flinterman
Professor of Human Rights, Utrecht University, Director of the Netherlands Institute of Human Rights and the Netherlands School of Human Rights Research

Marc Henzelin
Lecturer in International Criminal Law, University of Geneva

Attendees

Jeffrey Herbst
Professor of Politics and International Affairs, Princeton University

Bert B. Lockwood
Distinguished Service Professor of Law and Director of the Urban Morgan Institute for Human Rights, University of Cincinnati College of Law

Stephen Macedo
Laurance S. Rockefeller Professor of Politics and The University Center for Human Values, and Director of the Program in Law and Public Affairs, Princeton University

Martha L. Minow
Professor of Law, Harvard Law School

Stephen P. Marks
François-Xavier Bagnoud Professor, Harvard School of Public Health

Diane F. Orentlicher
Law and Public Affairs Fellow, 2000-2001, Princeton University, and Professor of Law and Director of the War Crimes Research Office, American University

Stephen A. Oxman
Member of the Board of Directors, American Association for the International Commission of Jurists, and Former U.S. Assistant Secretary of State for European and Canadian Affairs

Jordan Paust
Law Foundation Professor, University of Houston Law Center

W. Michael Reisman
Myres S. McDougal Professor of International Law, Yale Law School

Leila Sadat
Professor of Law, The Washington University School of Law

Anne-Marie Slaughter
J. Sinclair Armstrong Professor of International, Foreign and Comparative Law, and Director of Graduate and International Legal Studies, Harvard Law School

Chandra Sriram
Research Associate, International Peace Academy

Princeton Project on Universal Jurisdiction Drafting Committee

M. Cherif Bassiouni, Chair
Professor of Law and President of the International Human Rights Law Institute, DePaul College of Law; Former Chair of the Drafting Committee of the United Nations Diplomatic Conference on the Establishment of the International Criminal Court

Christopher L. Blakesley
(November only)
J.Y. Sanders Professor of Law at the Paul M. Hebert Law Center Louisiana State University

William J. Butler
Former Chairman of the Executive Committee of the International Commission of Jurists, 1975-1990, and President of the American Association for the International Commission of Jurists

Stephen Macedo
Laurance S. Rockefeller Professor of Politics and The University Center for Human Values; Director of the Program in Law and Public Affairs, Princeton University

Diane F. Orentlicher
Law and Public Affairs Fellow, 2000-2001, Princeton University, and Professor of Law and Director of the War Crimes Research Office, American University

Stephen A. Oxman
Member of the Board of Directors, American Association for the International Commission of Jurists, and Former U.S. Assistant Secretary of State for European and Canadian Affairs

Lloyd L. Weinreb
(November only)
Dane Professor of Law, Harvard Law School

Acknowledgments

Thanks to our institutional sponsors for providing the resources to make this Project possible. Thanks also to all of our official participants and attendees and all others who furnished comment on the Principles at various stages.

The Drafting Committee also acknowledges the tireless efforts of Steven W. Becker (J.D., DePaul University College of Law, June 2001), Sullivan Fellow, International Human Rights Law Institute, of the DePaul College of Law, who served as research assistant to Professor Bassiouni and as rapporteur to the Drafting Committee of the Princeton Project.

Many people at Princeton University, especially in the Woodrow Wilson School of Public and International Affairs, helped plan and organize the two meetings of the Princeton Project on short notice. David Figueroa-Ortiz, Chandra Sriram, and Simon P. Stacey provided crucial organizational support. Thanks also to Betteanne Bertrand and Sally Buchanan for their flexibility and careful attention.

Scott Wayland made essential editorial contributions while this volume was in preparation. Laurel Masten Cantor provided crucial production expertise. Thanks most of all to Cynthia Kinelski for going above and beyond the call of duty to pull together all of the practical details without which our meetings would not have run smoothly.